# REAL WORLD SUPERPOWERS

## SUCCESS PRINCIPLES FOR THE NEXT GENERATION

Liz Lequeux

Copyright © 2025 by Liz Lequeux
All rights reserved.

Published by Liz Lequeux
www.lizleq.com

Editing and layout by Paul Braoudakis

ISBN: 979-8-9925490-3-4

All rights reserved. No part of this book may be reproduced or transmitted in any form or by any means, electronic or mechanical, including photocopying and recording, or by an information storage and retrieval system, without permission in writing from the author. This includes reprints, excerpts, photocopying, recording, or any future means of reproducing text.

Printed in the United States of America

# DEDICATION

To my Lilly girl. You already have all the sparkle within you to live a happy, successful, and fulfilling life. I've watched you accomplish anything you wanted when you set your mind to it, even when the going got tough, you kept going. I am proud of you! I love you and I believe in you.

To my Lucas. One of the many things I love and admire about you is that you always want to do what's right. I am so proud of you! You have incredible drive and will be wildly successful. Keep on inspiring the world with your talents. I love you very much.

To my Maxwell. You light up the room when you walk in! Keep smiling and being you, spreading your love to the world. In first and second grade, both teachers independently gave you The Mindset Award. That's the best award one can win in life. I love you. You're my heart.

David, my soulmate, you are my hero and my guide. Through thick and thin, I'm grateful to go through this adventure called life together!

Mom, thank you for always believing in me and encouraging me to be the best. You are an amazing, courageous, and beautiful woman.

Dad, thank you for loving me unconditionally no matter what. You always had my back in ups and downs and I knew it would be safe for me to take wings and fly. You are the sweetest man I know.

To my editor, Paul, I have learned so much. You are a great man of character.

# PURPOSE

I've led thousands of people and have spoken to stadium-sized crowds. Yet, I struggled to find a topic so important to write a book about — until now. This book is a love letter to YOU, the next generation of leaders in this world. I want you to know that you are deeply loved and to recognize your worth. You can make a positive impact in the lives of others! This book is filled with secrets about life, love, relationships, success, and money that I've discovered and wish to pass on. My hope is to encourage you daily to live a happy and fulfilled life.

The most impactful book that set me up for success was the first personal development book I ever read: *The 10 Things I Wish I'd Known Before I Entered The Real World* by Maria Shriver. My mother gave it to me as a high school graduation gift and what a gift it was.

That book started my journey in the personal growth arena and has been the catalyst to a successful, happy, and fulfilling life. I wish that everyone who reads this book experiences the same transformative impact.

# INTRODUCTION

## Unleash Your Inner Superhero

Picture your favorite superhero. What do you love most about them? Do you love that they have courage in the face of tremendous hurdles? Do you admire how they keep their cool when the villain talks trash?

In life, you will face moments that require you to channel your inner superhero – to overcome obstacles, deal with difficult people, go for the promotion, and step into your greatness.

In these situations, what's more important than learning what to do is learning how to think. Do you know people who are constantly negative, quick to criticize, and always complain about being stuck? On the flip side, do you know people who love life, are positive, and successful in everything they do? What's the difference between the two? The philosophies they learned and the mindset they chose to adopt.

Together we will help you develop a winning mindset for success, open doors to opportunities, give you the tools to build happy relationships, and become a great leader. We will help you discover your purpose and even teach you how to identify your soulmate when you meet them.

Are you ready to unleash your inner superpowers?
Let's get started!

# SUPERPOWER INDEX

BELIEVE IN YOURSELF → 1

DON'T TAKE IT PERSONALLY → 9

OWN IT → 21

JUMP IN → 27

THE POWER OF YOUR THOUGHTS → 39

THE POWER OF RIZZ → 49

THE RULES OF MONEY → 57

SPEAK UP → 65

DATING SUPERPOWERS → 75

YOUR SUPERHERO SQUAD → 85

DREAMS → 93

YOUR UNIQUE SUPERPOWER → 105

COMMENCEMENT SPEECH → 115

# 1

# Believe in Yourself

*"There's never been another you in this world, and there never will be, so go be the best YOU you can be!"*
-Jamie Kern Lima, Author of *Worthy*

Have you ever thought, "Am I good enough?"

"Will they like me?"

"What if I mess up?"

If you're like me, you've most likely had those thoughts. Everyone is slightly insecure. It doesn't matter if you're popular or famous. We all experience moments of doubt and worry about what others think of us. The funny thing is, they're usually not thinking about us at all — they're too busy worrying about themselves and what others are thinking of them.

Sometimes I get sucked into worrying about what people will think of me on social media. Before I hit the "share" button, I often think, "Are people going to like this? Will they think it's stupid?"

Many times I look at the picture I'm about to post and think, "I should retake this, my face looks too fat/ pale/ double chin …" You name it, I've worried about it!

Then I remember that others are also worried about the same thing, so what's the point of worrying at all? Let's all just be ourselves! Start believing in yourself and shift your focus from worrying about others' opinions to showing compassion for others as fellow humans experiencing the same struggles.

## Believe in yourself even when others don't

Did you know that Walt Disney was fired from a newspaper job because they said he "lacked imagination and had no good ideas?" Disney went on to create one of the most incredible entertainment empires in the world. You have to believe in yourself, even when others don't.

I had to learn how to believe in myself when I started my business. Many friends thought it was too risky, and that I should just get a safe, secure job. They thought I was nuts.

One night, I went out with my friends for dinner and my best friend brought her new man for all of us to meet. She went around the table introducing us to him, and when she got to me he said, "Oh, you're the one doing the silly business!"

I laughed it off and said "Yeah, that's me!" but the whole rest of the night I was boiling with shame and embarrassment. Sitting there as everyone kept socializing around me with my eggplant parm barely eaten, I couldn't help but think, "Was my dream really stupid and unrealistic? Do others think this about me, too?" Obviously she was mocking me behind my back or he would have never said that. She was my best friend! I thought she would be positive and supportive with everything I did.

## If you don't know how to believe in yourself, believe in your mission

Despite the insults I had to face, I knew my mission was strong. I read somewhere that "If what you do comes from a place of love, you can do no wrong." My company's mission was about helping people and I believed that if I stuck to that mission it would work ... and years later it did — to the tune of helping 67,000 customers nationwide through my agency to date.

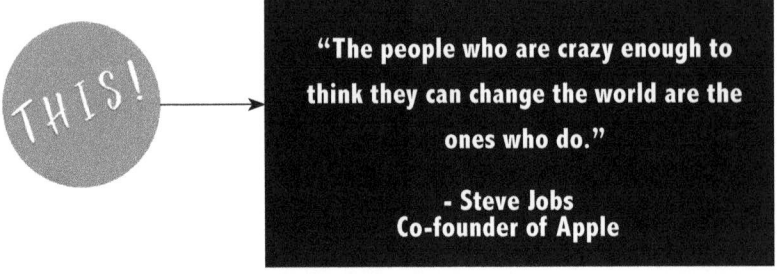

"The people who are crazy enough to think they can change the world are the ones who do."

- Steve Jobs
Co-founder of Apple

So, never second-guess yourself. Believe in yourself that you can do good in this world, even if others don't see it yet. Believe in your mission, especially if it involves helping people. If God puts a desire, a dream, or an idea within you, then go for it! Just try, and if you don't succeed the first time, try again! It took Thomas Edison over 1,000 attempts to get the lightbulb right. Friends and family thought he was nuts. So stay encouraged, believe in yourself, and persevere.

## Believe in yourself when opportunities come your way

When I was a junior in high school, I almost passed up an opportunity I would have deeply regretted. At the time, I was dating a boy named Steve. He was handsome, driven, and had the dream of being Student Council President. His dad was the dean of admissions at Princeton University and told him that if he got the role of President, it would greatly increase the chances for him to get into Princeton. I also dreamed of running for President because I was very involved in the club, in charge of all the school dances and spirit activities; but I didn't want to get in his way. Everything was going great. Our relationship really felt like it was going somewhere. But just as the campaign began, he decided to break up with me. He said he wanted to focus on school and the election. I was heartbroken.

Later that night, I was trying to do my homework and the lead tip of my mechanical pencil kept breaking. I couldn't concentrate and was really bummed out. Then it dawned on me:

*Now that we aren't together anymore, should I run for the position, too? No, he would hate me for it!*

I feared that it would stop him from ever wanting to get back together. I worried what everyone was going to think of me running against him. *I better not humiliate myself*, I thought. *No! Don't think about it.*

But I couldn't stop thinking about it! I couldn't ignore the voice inside my head telling me that this was a once-in-a-lifetime chance because I'd never be in high school again! I loved the student council and everything this role would be responsible for.

So I decided, "I'm going to go for it! He is the one who broke up with me. Why should I care what he thinks anymore? IT'S GAME ON!"

It was very last minute and I was the last to enter the race. (I swear I wasn't doing it to spite him, but I was definitely going to enjoy beating him.)

Whether I won or not, it was a great experience. I learned how to step outside my comfort zone, make new friends, talk to kids I never spoke to before, and give it my all. Taking this chance turned out to be a lot of fun!

Then came election day. My heart raced as they announced the winner. I couldn't believe it … they announced my name! Here was something I just had a last-minute inspiration to do, and as a result of trying and learning to believe in myself, I had won! What if I didn't listen to the voice inside of me saying, "Go for it!"?

(Steve still got into Princeton, all was happy.)

> We must embrace the opportunities that come our way. The more we go for them, our confidence grows

Believe in yourself because you are a child of God. The only person's opinion of us that we should care about is His. He created you to be uniquely YOU, capable of doing things only you can do! *By stepping out and doing your thing, you'll inspire others to do the same.*

# 2

# Don't Take It Personally

*"What you think about me is none of my business."*
-Anthony Hopkins, Actor

We all want others to like us. It's just how we're wired. I want to give you a heads-up that there will be times in your life when people say or do mean things to you. When this happens, as personal as it may feel, I encourage you not to take it personally.

One time, I had to do this when a friend made a mean comment about my profile picture on Facebook. It came out of nowhere. I thought we were friends! I wasn't expecting him to say that at all. He called me "fake." It hurt me because I've been striving to be the most sincere and caring person to everyone I meet. More than 200 friends made positive, loving comments but all I could focus on was the one negative comment.

I thought of a million different things to say back to him. I wanted to send him a private message and tell him how hurt I was. I drafted and deleted the message several times. Before I hit "Send," I remembered what I read in John Maxwell's book *Winning with People,* where he teaches "The Hurting People Principle." He explains that "hurting people hurt people and are easily hurt by other people." This means that when someone says something mean to you, don't take it personally, because usually, it's not about you. It's about the hurt they're feeling inside from something happening to them in their world that's causing them to respond in mean and hurtful ways. Happy people don't say mean things to others; only those who are hurting do.

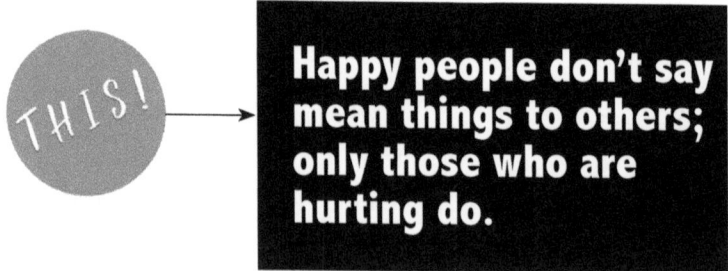

So, instead of sending my friend a strong message, I decided to go to his Facebook profile and see what was happening in his life. His wife was suffering from cancer. He was in a very hard place. I thought she had been healed; I didn't know she was still going through the battle. I immediately went from taking offense to feeling compassionate. I hadn't seen him in years or interacted on social media all this time because it only showed me some friends' posts, and not everyone's. Instead of responding with anger, I decided to send him some love. I happened to see a donation link on his page to help his business and I made a donation. Whether he noticed it or not, it didn't matter anymore. Responding with love made me feel better. If someone hurts you and you respond with love and understanding, it will leave you with a feeling of peace instead of anger.

He eventually came back and said he was sorry about his comment and that he was in a really bad mood at the time. My happy picture was the first thing he saw and he wasn't in his right mind. Today we love and respect each other and have even supported one another in each other's businesses. However, if I had responded with anger or had taken it personally, I don't think our relationship would be where it is today.

The next time someone says something or does something that hurts you, try to remember not to take it personally. It's usually not about us, it's what's happening with them. Going a step further and showing love to them, even when you feel they don't deserve it, can break down barriers and walls.

*"Do not repay evil with evil ... instead repay it with good."*
(Romans 12:17-21)

Have the courage not to take things personally and try to understand where the other person is coming from. It requires more strength to do this, but it will bring you more peace in the end.

## Social Media and Friends

Social media can be a tricky place to be sometimes when it comes to friendships. One day, I was scrolling through my Facebook feed and saw a picture of my old college roommates standing in Times Square. It looked like they got together for a drink and had a little reunion. Everyone looked amazing and it was so good to see their smiling faces. Then it dawned on me that the only person missing from this picture was me! I assumed it was a simple oversight because I live in California and they all live on the East Coast, so I immediately dropped the comment, "Omg! Hey girls!! You all look amazing! I'm so happy to see your smiling faces!"

When no one replied to it, I assumed they were not very active on social media and didn't think anything of it.

The next year rolled around and I saw another post with all the same college roommates ... this time in a tropical location. I immediately thought "Wow, how neat! They're starting to get together. I would love to come and see everyone again! They must have forgotten to invite me this year, or maybe I missed a message somewhere." I immediately checked my inbox for a possible message from each one and saw nothing.

In this year's picture, they were joined by another friend we all used to hang out with, so I messaged her. She replied right away and we started messaging back and forth having fun catching up after all these years. Finally, I asked about their recent get-together and told her how amazing I thought it was that everyone was starting to get together. Then she told me, "The girls get together every year! They have been for the last 20 years."

Uhhh, what did she just say? 😯 😮 😱 😨 👻 😰 ☹️ 😡

The girls have been getting together all these years and never once thought to invite me? *And* they posted the picture? A million thoughts ran through my head ...

What did I do that made them want to exclude me? Didn't we all get along really well? Did they just forget? And forgot when they posted? We had so many fun times together! Did I do something to offend someone?

I was so hurt. It affected me for weeks. I reached out to each one individually to connect and some responded back with a nice hello, but I didn't have the guts to bring up the reunions.

Every time I share this with someone I usually hear things like:

"It's probably because you live in the West and they all live in the East."

"They probably just wanted to get wasted and they know you don't really do that."

"You've become so successful, they probably think you don't want to come."

Whatever the excuse is, I've had to learn that not everyone is going to like you and not everyone will remember to invite you even if they do like you. I know they did not intentionally mean to hurt me.

The truth is, when I moved to California I lost touch and I could have done better on my part to stay connected to each one of them all these years. I was so wrapped up in my new life that I did not. I knew this, but it still hurt. This is why social media can be tricky.

I've also been on the flip side where I unintentionally hurt people on social media. I get busy sometimes and don't have a chance to respond to people who like and comment on my posts. One day I was checking my Messenger app on Facebook and discovered I had more than 100 messages from people I never responded to in a "Message Requests" folder because Facebook filtered them out as spam! Oh, my godness, I felt so bad not answering these friends! Especially since I knew how bad it feels to be ignored on social media.

## Don't take things personally on social media because social media is not personal

Social media is a great way to meet new friends and stay in touch with old ones you may never have seen again. But it's not always real. Most people just post the highlights of their life, not the lowlights. Most people don't post the challenges they're going through. So we don't really know the depths of them. It's surface level and hard to feel close to someone when we only know part of them, and not the whole story.

The best way to judge the quality of your friendships is by looking at the ones you have right now. The friends you see regularly, in person, or on the phone.

## Sometimes God Turns Your Pain Into Your Purpose

Because of these painful experiences, I have made it my mission to make people feel loved, accepted, valued, and included. I try not to ignore anyone who reaches out as much as I can. My life's purpose is to be the "Chief Encouragement Officer" to everyone in my life, to uplift, motivate, and encourage those who come into my path.

## Be The Bigger Person

Many times in life, you'll need the courage to "be the bigger person." This means choosing to act with maturity and kindness, even when it's difficult. Whether you're in an argument with a loved one or assisting a disgruntled customer at work, learn to be the first to say, "I'm sorry."

"I'm sorry" are the most powerful words you can use in relationships, even if it's not your fault. You're probably thinking, *how in the world does this make me powerful if I'm giving the power to the other person?* Saying "I'm sorry" doesn't mean you're weak; it actually means you're strong.

To say "I'm sorry" to someone says to them "I hear you, I understand you, and I can see you feel upset." In relationships, it's not about being right, it's more important that you reconcile and learn how to get along.

You can still express your point of view and share how you're feeling. It's just that sometimes the other person won't be willing to hear your side of the story until you get the courage to be the bigger person and say "I'm sorry" first.

I know of marriages that have broken up because one person wouldn't say they're sorry. It's so important to learn how to be the bigger person, especially if it means saving your marriage!

I've had to say "I'm sorry" to customers to calm them down, even when they were in the wrong. Recently a customer was being disruptive at one of our locations, making it really hard for all the other customers to enjoy their experience. Our manager politely asked him to tone it down, but that made him really mad and he decided to tone it up! He started shouting and yelling making a big stink. I immediately went over and apologized for the situation. I said, "I am so sincerely sorry for the way you were treated." I listened to him, and as he expressed himself, he started to calm down. Apologizing helps others feel their feelings are acknowledged.

The next time you're in a heated situation that requires you to be the bigger person:

**Stay Calm:** When someone is rude or mean, instead of reacting with anger, stay calm and composed.

**Show Empathy:** Understand that others might be going through tough times. Show compassion instead of judgment.

**Forgive:** Let go of grudges and forgive others, even if they haven't apologized.

**Take Responsibility:** Own up to your mistakes and make things right.

**Lead by Example:** Act in a way that sets a positive example for others to follow.

Have the courage to be the bigger person. Rise above the drama and choose to respond with kindness and respect.

> *"Be kind and compassionate to one another, forgiving each other, just as in Christ God forgave you."*
> (Ephesians 4:32)

# 3

# Own it!

*"You get to take credit in life for all the things you do right as long as you take responsibility for all the things you do wrong. It must be a balanced equation."*

-Simon Sinek, Author of *Start With Why* and *Leaders Eat Last*

There was a period of time when I blamed my husband for keeping me up all night with his snoring. It was so loud it would ricochet against the windows. I would get cranky with him the next day and tell him it was his fault that I had a bad night's sleep. He felt bad but he didn't know how to control it. This went on for weeks. Some nights I would get nice and comfy in my bed, my body would start to relax, and I'd begin to drift off to sleep ... and then Zzzzzzzzzzzzzz!

Then one day it dawned on me that I had the power to change the situation. I stopped pointing my finger at him and took the problem into my own hands. I made sure to stop looking at my phone screen one hour before bed, I drank "sleepy time" tea, and I ordered lawn mower ear muffs from Amazon ... yes, the kind of ear muffs the guys who drive the big lawn mowers wear! I took full responsibility for the situation. Now when he snores, I can't hear him and I sleep like a baby.

Jack Canfield, the author of *Success Principles*, says, "Take 100% responsibility for everything that you experience in your life." This means you have to give up blaming others for the circumstances you're in today. You're in it because you decided to stay in it. The word "blame" itself stands for *B-lame*. You have the power to change things starting now.

## Take Responsibility For Your Feelings and Your Life

Maybe something awful really did happen to you. I am so sorry you went through that. You are a warrior. It's OK to have feelings of disappointment, anger, or betrayal. However, I want to empower you with a word of advice: Continuing to blame others for the way you're feeling is only going to keep you feeling powerless. That's because you're putting your fate in the hands of others to make it right.

My incredible friend, mentor, and self-made millionaire, Elizabeth Gardner, says, "The person who broke you isn't coming back to fix you." So stop waiting for others to make things right because you have the power to change it and make your life what you want it to be starting now.

Did you know people only complain about the things they have the power to change? I have a friend who always complains about her job and her boyfriend every time I see her. She talks about all the things he does wrong and complains about everything her co-workers do that bugs her. If she hates it that much, why does she stay? Sometimes people can't see the light at the end of the tunnel because they're trapped in the dark.

> *"If you don't like how things are, change it.*
> *You are not a tree!"*
> -Jim Rohn, the world's leader in self-improvement

## You Can Change The Trajectory Of Your Future

We are always living in the results of our past thoughts and actions. If you spent all your money, then today you're broke. But if you start saving money, you will eventually live abundantly. If you pissed off all your friends by being mean, you are alone. But if you start planting seeds of kindness, tomorrow you'll be surrounded by wonderful friendships.

## You Get To Choose

Every day you get to choose if it's going to be a great day or a bad day. Each time something happens to you, you get to choose whether to react positively or negatively to it. When someone says something that upsets you,

you get to choose whether you're going to let it ruin your day or not.

My friend Jenny's mother was very verbally abusive to her. She would insult her regularly and never apologized. Naturally, Jenny got offended and angry right away. She would stew about it and think about what she should have said back. Jenny would let it ruin her entire day.

On other days, she paused to consider that her mom had grown up with an abusive father and dealt with daily struggles of depression. Remembering this side of her mom, Jenny's heart shifted from anger to compassion. She felt sympathy for her mom. Although her mother's verbal abuse was not acceptable, it allowed Jenny to view the situation from a different perspective. Instead of letting it ruin her entire day, she was able to forgive and move on, and the rest of her day went peacefully as planned.

When upsetting things happen to us, we get to choose whether we are going to let it get the best of us or we can choose to let it go and rise above the situation.

## The 30-Second Rule

My coach, David Byrd, teaches a technique called The 30-Second Rule. Anytime you're faced with an obstacle or a problem, set a timer for 30 seconds. During those 30 seconds, you can scream, cry, stomp your feet, and stew about the situation. But when the alarm goes off, you gotta get up and get going! He says "Start writing a 'Can-Do' list." This is a list of solutions that you can do to solve your problem.

When you take responsibility for everything that happens in your life, you will feel how truly powerful it is to own it.

> *"Until you take ownership for your life,*
> *you will always be chasing happiness."*
> –Sean Stephenson

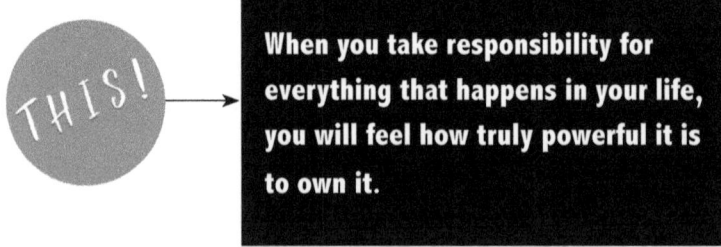

# 4

# Jump In

*"You don't have to see the whole staircase, just take the first step."*
-Martin Luther King

Halle Bailey, who plays Ariel in the newest "The Little Mermaid" movie, got her start in the entertainment industry by posting cover songs of her and her sister, Chloe, singing on YouTube. People liked their music, which eventually caught the attention of Beyoncé. Halle and Chloe were eventually signed to Beyoncé's record label in 2015, and in 2023 Halle starred in "The Little Mermaid." Just think, if Halle and her sister never put their singing videos out there, they may never have been discovered.

Billie Eilish started making music as a teenager in her bedroom. She didn't know how she was going to make it big. She didn't have a professional studio to record her first song or access to a big record label to help her. She just knew she had a passion for music and was willing to try. She first released her music on SoundCloud, a platform where anyone from amateur to professional musicians can share their work. She kept going, and then she got noticed. Today, she has won multiple Grammy Awards and is one of the most popular singer-songwriters. Billie's journey shows that you don't need to have everything figured out from the start, you just need to start.

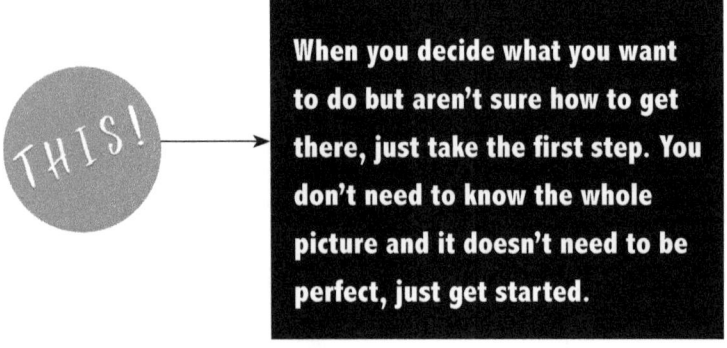

**When you decide what you want to do but aren't sure how to get there, just take the first step. You don't need to know the whole picture and it doesn't need to be perfect, just get started.**

## Just Get In Motion

Tony Robbins, the #1 motivational speaker in the world, says, "Motion creates positive emotion." I found this to be true at work. I had mentors in my company tell me that all I had to do to be successful was share our services with two people a day. Sounded simple enough, but guess which of the two was the hardest to do? The first one of the day! The phone felt like it weighed a thousand pounds, but the second call only felt like one pound. I just had to get through the first one. Some days, I didn't feel like doing it, but I'd force myself to make the calls, and suddenly I'd feel better. The earlier in the day I took action, the better I felt about myself. Each day, it got easier to take action, and by consistently taking action, I began to consistently make sales.

The opposite was true for me, too. There were days when I avoided making calls. If I stayed stagnant too long, negative emotions would start to creep in. I'd begin to doubt myself, get stressed out by the workload piling up, and then have to muster up even more courage than I originally needed, and it was not fun.

Brendon Burchard's "Law of Congruence" states: "If you're not doing what you know you should be doing it leads to self-loathing." *The more we procrastinate, the worse we will feel about ourselves.*

What have you been putting off that you can start on today?

## Where Does Motivation Come From?

Most people make the mistake of thinking motivation comes before the action. They say, "I'll go to the gym when I feel like it," or "I'll start that project when I'm feeling ready." However, successful people will tell you that what makes them so successful is they do things even when they don't feel like it.

I met the late basketball star Kobe Bryant while working out at my old gym when I lived in Orange County. Every day I was there, he was there with his trainer either lifting, doing the StairMaster, or shooting hoops. It seemed as if every time I went to the gym, whether it was morning, afternoon, or evening, he was there. I'm sure there were days when he didn't feel like doing it, but doing it consistently is what made him so successful. He was one of the greatest legends in basketball history.

He was a beautiful soul with a kind, warm smile, and a big heart.

Dwayne "The Rock" Johnson faced numerous challenges and setbacks before becoming a successful actor. After his dreams of becoming a professional football player were smashed due to injuries, he turned to wrestling. Even when he didn't feel like it, he pushed through the tough times, trained relentlessly, and eventually became one of the most famous wrestlers in the world. His perseverance and hard work led to a successful career in Hollywood as the A-list star we know him as today.

When it comes to work, I don't always feel like doing it. But after making the first few calls, I suddenly feel happy that I'm doing it! The more I do it, the easier it gets, and then I don't even have to think about it — it just becomes part of my daily routine.

Motivation doesn't always come before taking action. It usually comes after taking action. Just take the first step and you'll start to feel excited to do more.

> *"Do the thing and then you'll have the power."*
> -Ralph Waldo Emerson, philosopher

## Consistency Is Your Friend

Every day, we get to choose whether or not to do something positive toward our goals.

I admire my son Lucas who started his YouTube Channel for gamers one year ago. He decided to post one video a day of him teaching tricks on how to get through tough levels of different games. At first, he didn't get very many views, but as he stayed consistent, posting one new video every day, he started gaining traction. Every day after school he'd throw his backpack down, run up the stairs, and record. He never missed a day. Now when he posts a new video, some get more than 10,000 views.

Ed Mylett is a famous YouTuber and the host of The Ed Mylett Show. My friend Jennifer knew Ed when he was just getting started and said he was dedicated to posting one video a week to build his show. He did it every week even when he didn't feel like doing it. Because of his consistency, he has built a channel with over a million subscribers and written a best-selling book, *The Power of One More*.

Our lives are made up of thousands of little decisions we've made over the years that have given us the results we have today. If we've eaten healthy for years, we feel strong, energetic, and vibrant today. If we've eaten junk for years, we feel sluggish, moody, and out of shape. This applies to every part of our lives: health, relationships, spirituality, money, career, and mental wellness.

Jeff Olsen birthed a concept called "The Slight Edge." It basically means that small daily choices we make compound over time and either lead to massive success or to failure. It's based on the idea that success is not the result of a single big effort, but really the result of many small, disciplined actions over time that add up to a lot.

Let's say, for instance, you save $1 every day. At the end of the year, you have $365 extra dollars saved up. One dollar seems like nothing but the slight edge of saving it daily gives you $365.

Let's make that $10 every day. By the end of the year, you've saved $3,650. Keep doing it consistently for the next 10 years and you'll save $36,500. That's enough for a down payment on a starter home or investment property!

What if you want to get ripped for the summer? Do 10 push-ups every day and by summer time you're ripped!

**Here's the thing: Every day you wake up, you have to make the decision to do it again.**

*Every day you have to decide to save the dollar.*

*Every day you have to decide to do the push-ups.*

*Every day you have to decide to go to work.*

It's not like you can make the decision one time and set it on autopilot. You have to make the choice every day.

Decisions seem small in the act of doing them, but the right ones made consistently over time will give you the results you're looking for.

The slight edge is also true for negative decisions. When I was in college, I made the mistake of opening up a credit card (different from a debit card that uses money from your bank account). I didn't have a job, so whatever I put on my credit card, I didn't have enough to pay it back. This was not a smart idea. I started buying clothes and shoes with money I didn't have. When the bill came each month, I couldn't pay the full amount. I only paid the minimum which is a very bad financial decision (more on that in "The Rules of Money" chapter). I continued to make these seemingly small purchases on the credit card. A shirt here, a pair of jeans there, going out to eat with friends ... and then, four years later when I graduated, I had accumulated $40,000 of credit card debt! This was not good at all!

The good news is I was able to pay it off after long years of doing the slight edge on the positive side of money. I started a home-based business to make extra income in addition to my job and used that money to pay off the cards. The moral of the story is: Little decisions we make consistently over time will compound and either improve our lives or come back to bite us in the end! If you don't like where you're at today, you can change it starting right now!

Once you embark on your journey to success, you might not see results right away. I want to encourage you that if you're making good decisions consistently, your success is growing even when you don't think it is! It's like a seed in the ground that's growing roots. You can't see the sprouts yet, but it's growing! One year later, you'll have a watermelon, but right now all you see is dirt!

## 21 Days To Form A Good Habit

Forming a good habit takes time and consistency. You've probably heard that it takes 21 days to form a new habit. This idea comes from Dr. Maxwell Maltz, who noticed that it took about 21 days for his patients to get used to something new. By sticking to your new routine for at least three weeks, you can start to make the new habit a natural part of your daily life. The more you stick to it, the easier it becomes, and soon enough, it will feel like second nature.

*"Be like a postage stamp. Stick to it until you arrive."*
- Josh Billings, American humorist

Last year I wanted to lose 10 pounds in time for the beach. I decided I would do it by cutting out the three major inflammatory foods from my diet: gluten, dairy, and sugar, all known to cause weight gain. They were not easy to avoid because those ingredients seemed to be in everything. Instead of ordering a hamburger at the drive-thru, I changed my habit to getting it lettuce-wrapped style. Instead of getting ice cream when I felt like having sweets, I changed the habit to eating strawberries, bananas, grapes, and pineapples.

To help me stay on track, I made a habit-tracking sheet (see link to the FREE tracker at the end of this chapter.) On the left column, I wrote down, "No sugar, no gluten, no dairy." To the right of each habit, I could check the box for each day of the month when I made it through the day without eating it. I also wrote down "cardio" to make sure I did my cardio five days a week. I added "2 exposures" to make sure I reached out to two new potential clients a day.

The first week, I only had a few check marks. The second week, I had more, and the third week I scored 100%. Each day that went by, my ability to make healthier choices got easier. It took about 21 days for me to turn each one into a habit. Now I'm not even interested in sugar, gluten, or dairy anymore. I couldn't believe it because they were my weakness! My body has healed itself from inflammation and, yes, I lost 10 pounds!

Stay encouraged knowing you're on your way, doing the little things to make it happen every day.

> *"Do not grow weary in doing good, for at the right time you will reap a harvest if you do not give up."*
> - Galatians 6:9

 Download the FREE Habit Tracker from www.LizLeq.com to stay on track with your goals and keep your daily decisions top of mind.

# 5

# The Power Of Your Thoughts

*"Successful leaders don't teach their teams what to do, they teach them how to think."*
-Liz Lequeux

How do you think? Positive and negative thoughts constantly flow through our minds. But be careful — whatever you spend time thinking about, you attract more of. For example, if you constantly think about how much you dislike school, you'll likely find more reasons to be unhappy there. On the other hand, if you focus on the things you enjoy, like hanging out with friends or participating in your favorite activities, you'll start to notice more positive aspects of your school experience.

If you spend your time worrying about the lack of money, you'll find more reasons why you can't afford things. However, if you focus on thinking "How can I afford this?" your mind will get creative and find ways to make the money and achieve your goals.

## Think Like The Owner

My very first job was working for the mafia. Or at least I think they were. I was a waitress at the most popular pizza restaurant in New Jersey. My bosses were three brothers Jeremy, Andrew, and Anielo. They were very fatherly and protective of me. Anytime guys would come in and try to talk to me, they would stand over them with their arms folded and look down at them with a smirk. I'd joke and tell my friends they were the mafia because they were the sweetest big teddy bears to me and then they'd walk back into the kitchen and you could hear them shout at each other and crash dishes against the wall as the brothers fought at least once a week. It was a fun job.

They'd say, "Liz, if you want to be successful in life, you've got to think like the owner!"

To get to the top in your company, don't think like an employee; think like the owner. The owner goes above and beyond to make customers happy, treats others with respect, and takes extra care of the store or business. That's how they became the owner. Jeremy, the oldest pizza brother, was always thinking of ways to improve things for the customers. He made sure every pizza, calzone, and cannoli was made with the highest quality ingredients. He was constantly inventing new foods — one day he created "garlic knots," and they became a nationwide hit! At your job, if you go the extra mile to help customers, show up early, keep the place tidy, and be a team player, your positive attitude can lead to promotions and a pay raise.

Do what you say you're going to do. If you say you'll call, then call. If you say you'll be there, be there. Avoid overcommitting just to please others. If you don't deliver on your promise, it could cost you. Your boss, customer, or friend will be more grateful when you're honest about your limitations so it doesn't jeopardize their project or deadline.

While everyone else might be thinking like an employee and putting in minimal effort, think like the owner. You will stand out and go all the way to the top.

## Think Like The Minority

Society has taught people to think like the majority, but look at this chart:

**<u>95 % of the World vs. 5% of the World</u>**

Followers vs. Leaders

Consumers vs. Creators

Complainers vs. Innovators

Broke and Middle Class vs. Wealthy

Employee vs. Business Owner

Majority vs. Minority

If you want to be a leader, creator, innovator, or wealthy, then you'd better get used to being OK with being a minority! Not everyone is going to get you or understand you and that's OK. That's because superheroes don't fit in, they stand out!

## Where Do Positive Thoughts Come From?

It takes energy to be a leader; positive energy that comes from taking good care of your mental health and body. Jim Rohn, the world's leader in self-improvement, says to "Work harder on yourself than you do on your job."

## Hit The Gym

People ask me, "What's your secret to success in business?" and my answer always surprises them: "My secret to success in business is exercising first thing every morning." What does this have to do with high performance? A LOT! Exercise is not only good for your health and gives you energy, but it makes you happy. Exercise has been found to significantly decrease symptoms of depression.[1] What do you like to do for exercise? How can you add this to your daily routine?

## Water Is The New Wealth

Water is the new drink of the wealthy. Soda is for the uneducated. Too many studies and research show deterioration of health from sugary drinks[2] and nerve damage in the brain from artificial sweeteners in "zero sugar" drinks[3]. Our bodies are about 60% water. To keep things running smoothly, we need to drink water regularly because we lose it through activities like sweating and breathing.

---

1 National Institute of Health: The impact of exercise on depression: how moving makes your brain and body feel better - PMC
2 Centers for Disease Control and Prevention CDC: Rethink Your Drink: The Health Risks of Sugary Beverages - Franklin County Free Press
3 Harvard Health: Could artificial sweeteners be bad for your brain? - Harvard Health

Dr. Daniel Amen, one of the most famous brain health experts, says that even slight dehydration can raise stress hormones, which can damage the brain over time. He suggests drinking at least 10 cups of water a day to keep the brain hydrated and functioning optimally. Dr. Amen's studies show that proper hydration can improve blood flow to the brain, which in turn can enhance your mood and cognitive function, potentially reducing symptoms of depression.[4]

So, why not give your body what it needs by drinking more water and avoiding soda to keep your brain happy?

## Nutrient Dense vs. Nutrient Deficient

What is nutrient dense food? It's foods that are full of vitamins and minerals like fruits, vegetables, and lean meats and fish. Nutrient deficient foods are void of vitamins and minerals, like pizza, hot dogs, and pasta. Although super tasty going down, it doesn't give you the best energy because you are not getting the vitamins and minerals your body needs. This is why we feel sluggish after eating pizza. Eat salmon, kale, and strawberries, and your body is buzzing with mental clarity and energy.

---

[4] Dr Amen: Seven Simple Brain-Promoting Nutritional Tips - Creativity at Work

Have you ever eaten several bowls of cereal, and your belly feels full, but you're still hungry? It's because your body is saying, "I need nutrients!" — nutrients you'll get from eating fruits, vegetables, and lean protein.

Nutrient-dense foods will help you feel your best. Not just your body, but your mental health. Without vitamins and minerals, you may feel irritated, agitated, sad, or have anxiety and can't figure out why. It's subtle, but having the right nutrients can seriously level up how you feel every day.

## Sleep

For young adults, sleep is incredibly important for your overall health and energy levels. According to the CDC, about 72% of high school students do not get the recommended eight hours of sleep per night.[5] Insufficient sleep in teens is found to cause mood swings and increased risk of mental health problems. Getting enough sleep can significantly improve your energy levels, focus, and overall well-being. So go to bed earlier!

---

[5] FastStats: Sleep in High School Students | Sleep | CDC

## Personal Development

In order to have positive thoughts, you need to be encouraged regularly. My friend Lou Moya listens to so many positive, motivational podcasts every day that I've seen him accomplish incredible feats, hit big goals, and overcome any challenge that comes his way. He has become attractive from the inside out and has become a great leader. He has the energy to encourage others because his cup overflows from the positivity he listens to every day. When he talks, so much positivity comes out because he's putting so much in.

The three places I have gotten great encouragement from are reading motivational books, attending church weekly, and reading the Bible. I've found really great advice about life and some of my favorite motivational quotes from the Bible. Pastor Ron Pierre says the Bible stands for **B**asic **I**nstructions **B**efore **L**eaving **E**arth. By reading a small passage every day, I am continually encouraged. It teaches me ways to grow in character, have better relationships, meet the spouse of my dreams, and live a life full of meaning, purpose, and joy.

> *"Blessed are all who hear the word of God*
> *and put it into practice."*
> -Luke 11:28

 **Get the "Leaders Academy" motivational audio for FREE on <u>www.LizLeq.com</u>.**
**Unlock inspiration, motivation and encouragement.**

# 6

# The Power Of Rizz (Charisma)

*"People will forget what you said, people will forget what you did, but people will never forget how you made them feel."*
- Maya Angelou

You've probably heard the term "rizz" when trying to get the girl. It comes from the word charisma. There are many definitions of charisma but here's my favorite one: The ability to make others feel good about themselves when they're around you. It's like having a magnetic charm that draws people in and makes them feel positive when they talk to you.

Charisma is often linked to being a great leader because it helps you influence and inspire others. I have an amazing friend, Kevin Torres, who is Mr. Charisma! He's like a big happy labrador who loves to see you and makes you feel like you're the most important person in the world! Every time we go on a business trip and everyone is responsible for their own travel, Kevin always goes out of his way to rent a car and pick every friend up from the airport that he can. He makes sure they have everything they need and he is always thinking how he can best help them. His wife, Linda, is Mrs. Charisma. She is the most thoughtful person I know! She is always showing genuine interest in people and always brings gifts when she sees you. She remembers people's birthdays and sends cards in the mail for every special life moment. They are both great leaders and everyone loves them.

My favorite leadership author, John Maxwell, says, "People only want to go along with those they get along with." This is so true! If you work on having a genuine interest in others, you can grow to be a great leader!

1. **Charisma Online**

We are living in a social media world. Everyone wants to be liked and accepted by others. What's interesting about social media is that those who have great self-esteem and are popular in real life will often post something on social media, and if no one likes it, they may second guess themselves. Unless you're a big influencer, most people's posts get very few likes, if any, and they wonder "does anybody see me?"

I have built a large social media following on Facebook by learning how to be a good friend. To be a good friend on social media means to encourage other people and cheer them on. Like and comment on people's posts when you see them. This says to them, "I see you, I understand you, I'm here for you!" When you like someone's post, they like you for noticing them. When you comment positively on their post, they'll love you for caring enough to engage.

People often ask me, "What should I post on social media?" They get intimidated and think being on social media is too hard. I want to relieve you of this anxiety by telling you it's not so important to figure out what to post. It's more important to like and comment on other people's posts to make them feel special about themselves. Cheer them on. That's what being friends in person is all about. Why should it be different online?

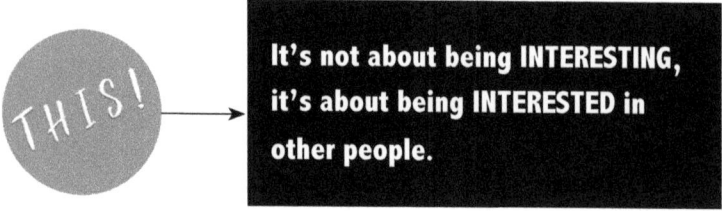

It's not about being INTERESTING, it's about being INTERESTED in other people.

This is the secret to success, life and relationships. This is what it means to have charisma.

## 2. Charisma Offline

In today's fast-paced digital world, it's easy to feel connected to tons of people but still feel lonely. With texting, Instagram, Tik-Tok, Discord, WhatsApp, Telegram, Snapchat, WeChat, Facebook Messenger, and more, we can connect with more people and start more conversations than ever before. But here's the thing — while texting and chatting on these apps are great for quick interactions, you can build deeper, more meaningful relationships offline. Magic happens when we hear each other's voices. You can say so much more on the phone.

My great friends, Nick and Tony Cifani, started their careers in health insurance in their early 20s and are now national sales leaders. Everyone who knows them loves these two brothers! What sets them apart is that they pick up the phone and call people. They don't just text or hide behind emails — they have real, human-to-human conversations. It's so refreshing when they call!

The emotional exchange you get from speaking to someone can't compare to a text message. On the phone, I can hear if they're feeling up or down. If they sound sad, I can ask if everything's OK and really hear how they're doing.

If I text someone, "How are you?" they might just say "Doing fine" even if they're not. They could be having a bad day and really need a friend to talk to, but I wouldn't know because they texted that they're fine!

It's easy to send a text or an email. It's not as easy to pick up the phone, but so much more happens when you do!

I have a rule that If I'm texting someone and we go back and forth more than five times, I just call them. You can get so much more done!

Emotions are hard to translate over text. I may write something that looks like I'm mad when I'm really excited because I like to use exclamation points!!!

## 3. Rizz in Leadership

**Ask Questions About Them**

When you ask others about themselves, it shows you care. I went on a date once with a guy where all he did was talk about himself. Womp womp! He never asked me questions about me. He was more interested in trying to impress me than getting to know me. I did not feel swept off my feet at all. When the date ended, he said he felt like he'd known me forever even though he knew nothing about me! When people get to talk about themselves, they feel more connected to you.

What questions should you ask? You can ask about their family, hobbies, work, and what they like to do for fun. My friend Sean Mikael likes to ask people, "What's good in your life today?" Once they answer the question, ask them a follow-up question. My friend Sallie Hasson likes to say, "Tell me more!"

**Be Fully Present**

People can tell if you're multitasking while you're talking to them. Listen deeply and try really hard not to look at your phone (I know it's hard!).

One time I interviewed a girl to be my personal assistant. She seemed very sweet, but every three minutes she looked at her phone and responded to every message that came in while we were talking. I remember thinking "If this is how she is when she is trying to get the job, how attentive will she be to my customers when she is on the job?"

Learning how to listen well takes time, so be patient with yourself! When I first started asking people, "How are you?" I was uncomfortable if their answer lasted longer than a minute. As I've matured, I have learned to love people and genuinely want to hear how they're doing. Now I love it when they go on and on!

**Are You A Lifter Or A Loader?**

I've seen good leaders and I've seen bad leaders. The best leaders make people feel better about themselves. The amateur leaders make them feel worse. Are you a lifter or a loader?

My business partner, A.J. DiLiberto, is one of the biggest lifters I know! He is full of charisma, telling everyone how much he believes in them and how amazing they are. He has something positive to pick out about each person he works with. While many other leaders like to point out people's flaws, A.J. is always telling people how amazing they are at their strength. I like to call him Coach A.J. because he cheers them on and has such a genuine interest in seeing them win.

My father-in-law, Blayne Lequeux, a leader in the men's leadership program "That Man Is You," says, "To be *charismatic* means to inspire others to follow Christ." To have love, joy, peace, patience, kindness, goodness, faithfulness, gentleness, and self-control (Galatians 5:22). Living with these qualities will naturally attract others to you.

*"Leading people is not about being interesting to them. It's about being interested in them."*
-Liz Lequeux

# 7

# The Rules Of Money

> "If you don't make a financial plan,
> you will make a spending plan."
> -Liz Lequeux

There's a saying "Money only makes you more of who you already are." If you're a nice person, money may allow you to be more generous to other people. If you're a mean person, money may make you more of a jerk. The most important thing you can do is work on your character first so when the money comes in, you'll be able to do great things.

## Money Rule #1 - Save 10% of every dollar you receive

If you earn $10, save $1.

If you earn $1,000, save $100.

If you learn how to save when you're earning small amounts of income, you'll be disciplined when you earn big amounts. People think, "When I earn more then I'll start saving." That's usually not the case. Unless you're in the habit of saving 10%, it's easy to fall into the trap of spending 100%.

Some employers have the ability to take a percentage of your paycheck and put it straight into your savings account. The rest goes into your checking account. Ask your company if you have this.

There are banking apps that help you save. With some, every purchase you make is rounded up to the nearest dollar, and the change is automatically transferred into your savings or investment account. It's a great way to save without even thinking about it!

*Why save money?* If you get in the habit of saving, you'll have money for the things you really want like renting your own apartment or buying that engagement ring. You'll have money for things you will need in an emergency like a flat tire or your dog that might need treatment at the vet and you can afford to save their life. If you don't save any money, your savings account will look just like the homeless person on the street!

Also, if you don't save money, you won't get to play at Level 2.

## Money Rule #2 - Invest

Remember the example of saving $10 every day for 10 years? You'll have $36,500 to put down on your first house.

If you invest that same $10 a day and it grows with compound interest of 10% per year, at the end of 10 years instead of having $36,500 you would actually have $94,676! You only put in $36,500 — that's free money! That's enough to buy two homes ... one to own and one to rent out to others for income. Now that sounds smart!

My mentor, the late Texan billionaire Paul J. Meyer, said, "Put overalls on your money!"

It wasn't until our family started saving and investing money that we were able to buy our home.

There are many different ways to invest. My uncle put $10,000 into Tesla stock in his granddaughter's name when she was born. By her 10th birthday, it had grown to $200,000. My husband's best friend invested in real estate and now owns 50 properties that pay a large monthly income. I invested in starting my own business, and my return has been millions of dollars and passive cash flow. Warren Buffett, one of the wealthiest men in America, recommends investing in the S&P 500[6]. He has often advised both beginner and advanced investors to choose low-cost S&P 500 index funds, such as the Vanguard S&P 500 ETF (VOO). He believes that these index funds offer a simple, effective way to achieve solid returns over the long term.

Make a *financial plan* to invest your money. Otherwise, when you have money coming in, you'll make a *spending plan*. "When I have extra money, I'll buy that BMW I've

---

[6] Warren Buffett's Golden Advice: S&P 500 Index Funds Reign Supreme For Retirement Success

been wanting," or "When we get extra money let's get that new couch we really need."

If you save and invest first, then whatever you have left over can be used for these things. Also, when your investments make you money you can use the profit to pay for these things.

> **Make a financial plan to invest your money. Otherwise, when you have money coming in, you'll make a spending plan.**

To gain more confidence about investing, start reading books about personal finance. My favorites are *Rich Dad, Poor Dad* by Robert Kiyosaki, *The Millionaire Next Door* by Thomas J. Stanley, *The Automatic Millionaire* by David Bach and *Money Mindset* by Brian Carruthers.

## Money Rule #3 - Just Don't Debt

As I mentioned earlier, when I was in college I made the mistake of getting into credit card debt. Everywhere

I turned, credit card offers were being handed to me! They came in the mail every week, they were offering credit cards outside my college cafeteria, and every time I flew on an airplane they were offering free miles if I signed up that day for a new credit card! Macy's, T.J. Maxx, and Old Navy gave me discounts for opening a credit card with them and continued to offer me bigger savings if I just used their card instead of using the money I had on my debit card every time I went shopping. This sounded like a good idea at first — save money on today's purchase by using the store credit card instead of the cash I had in my wallet! However, if you did not remember to pay it off in full within 30 days, you'd incur an interest fee, usually 25% of your purchase amount, which ended up costing more than the discount I got when I was trying to save money!

Interest on a credit card is a secret killer. Just like investing will compound your money, interest on a credit card can compound your debt. Also the credit card companies can be very sneaky and give you an introductory interest rate of 2% for one year, and then it jumps to 25% the second year! It's like playing with fire.

Every month the bills would come, I would cry! Fortunately, I started my home-based business on the side that I was able to make extra money with and have been able to pay off every penny of the debt. Even though I was able to get out of it, it was a very painful time I wish for no one to go through. So please, just don't start! Follow the rule and just don't debt and you will be happy.

## Money Rule #4 - Tithe (Give)

Tithing is when you set aside a portion of your money, usually, the first 10%, to give to your church or charity. It's a way of honoring God and trusting Him to provide for your needs. It's about being grateful for what you have and helping others. Giving helps your community and keeps you grounded in gratitude.

Giving money also helps you to be more prosperous. By sharing what you have, you open up space in your life for more blessings to flow in. It's like if you never picked the ripe fruit, the plant would stop producing new ones. By circulating your money, you're keeping the flow going.

Tithing is about developing the character of kindness and generosity, creating a positive cycle. When you give, you're not just helping others; you're also growing personally, building good habits, and often finding that life gives back to you in unexpected ways.

**Learning how money works firsthand will grow your character in so many ways. Follow these rules as your guide and you will feel abundant and prosperous.**

*"Bring the full tithe into the storehouse, that there may be food in my house. And thereby put me to the test, says the Lord of hosts, if I will not open the windows of heaven for you and pour down for you a blessing until there is no more need."*
(Malachi 3:10)

# 8

# Speak Up

*"Our lives begin to end the day we become silent about things that matter."*
-Martin Luther King Jr.

Your friends, family, and coworkers are not mind readers. If you're upset about something, don't assume they know how you're feeling. In this chapter, I'll show you how to share your feelings in an easy and healthy way.

My husband and I have been happily married for 16 years at the time of this publication, and we have never had a big fight. We think it's because we talk about our feelings right away. He calls me out as soon as I say something disrespectful, and I call him out as soon as he says something unloving. As long as we approach each other with care and don't wait too long, we can talk things out and come to an agreement.

## Speak Up Right Away

This approach works so well for us that even our kids have joined in. We are a family of five, and anytime one of us says something hurtful, someone immediately calls them out. The offender apologizes, and we quickly return to getting along.

My 7-year-old is the best at doing this! He's quick to say to the rest of the family, "Hey, you ate a bite of my pizza!" or "You said that in a mean voice," or "You scared me when you shouted at me!" Why is it that when we are young we share freely about how we feel but as we get older, we stuff it in?

## Don't Stuff It In

Have the courage to speak up when you need to share your feelings. If you feel hurt, don't hold it in. Address problems quickly so you can move on and spend more time being happy. The longer you wait to address the person who upset you, the longer you'll stew about it.

*If you're dealing with a difficult or abusive person, discuss the situation with a trusted authority first to talk about how you should handle it.*

## The SIG Method

Here's what I came up with that's helped me express my feelings with loved ones and coworkers over the years:

S:  State The Facts
I:  Use "I" Statements (Avoid blaming or using "You" statements.)
G: Give directions

**Example #1:** Your friend shares your personal secret without permission.

**S: *State The Facts:*** "Maddie said you told her what I shared with you in confidence."
**I: *Use "I" Statements:*** "I feel hurt because I trusted you with something very personal."

**G:  *Give Directions*:** "In the future, could you please keep my personal information confidential? It would mean a lot to me."

**Example #2:** You're in a group project, and one of your teammates hasn't been contributing much and it's weighing on the group.

**S:  *State The Facts:*** "I've noticed that you haven't been able to attend our last two group meetings and haven't submitted your part of the project yet."
**I:  *Use "I" Statements:*** "I feel really stressed because we're running out of time, and we need everyone's input to complete the project."
**G:  *Give Directions:*** "Could you please let us know if there's a reason you're unable to contribute? If you need help, we can figure out a way to support you. Otherwise, it would be great if you could work on your part and share it with us by tomorrow."

**Example #3:** Your roommate leaves dirty dishes in the sink often. It's making it hard for you to clean your own and it's stressing you out.

**S: State The Facts:** "I've noticed that you've been leaving dirty dishes in the sink for the past few days."

**I: Use "I" Statements:** "I feel frustrated because it's making the kitchen messy, and it's harder for me to cook and clean."

**G: Give Directions:** "Let's agree to clean our dishes within 24 hours so we can keep things clean and make our living space nice. Does that sound good to you?" You can even offer to have them tell you if there's anything you need to get better at to make your living together better.

The next time something happens and you don't feel good about it, have the courage to speak up. It will make you feel better and it will make your relationship with that person even closer because you can communicate openly and express how you feel.

## Say It Nicely

There's a famous saying that "You catch more flies with honey than with vinegar." This means that the nicer you ask for things or the more pleasant you are when you interact with people, the more agreeable they will be.

You may already know this, but when you're in the heat of the moment, it's not always easy to remember!

I was shoe shopping and there was a mom and her little boy in the store trying on shoe after shoe to find the perfect one. When they finally found the perfect pair they approached the counter and asked, "Is there a bathroom my son can use?"

The store clerk replied, "The closest restroom is at Target or Old Navy." Both of these stores were at least a five-minute walk across the big strip mall parking lot.

I could see the mom's temper boiling and she said, "Well what do you do when you have to go to the bathroom?"

The store clerk seemed innocent like she was just following her training, "Well, our restrooms are for employees only, but …"

The mom slammed down her boxes of shoes before the girl could finish, "Forget it! I'm not buying anything. Come on, Son, let's go somewhere else!"

When they left, the store clerk said to her coworker, "My goodness, she didn't have to cop an attitude with me. I was just about to tell her that I'm not allowed to do it, but just this once, I was going to let her son use our restroom quickly before the boss returns, but, oh well!"

I bet the mom is usually a nice person. She was under stress and forgot to be nice. But I imagine that after she found a restroom, if she wanted to come back to buy the shoes she worked so hard to find, she would be too embarrassed to return.

On one business trip to Hawaii, my flight arrived at 9 a.m. but the hotel where I was staying didn't allow check-ins until 4 p.m. I forgot about the later check-in time and I had a business meeting at 2 p.m. that I needed to shower and get dressed up for. It was the busiest hotel right on the beach in Waikiki and I could tell the front desk staff was stressed out with a long line of families demanding to be checked in early. When I got to the front, the receptionist looked frazzled and I said, "Hi! I just want to tell you that you're doing amazing. I see how hard you're working and how much you're juggling. How are you?"

She looked up from her computer in shock. She cracked a smile and said, "I'm hanging in there!" As she took my driver's license and debit card she explained that my room would not be ready until the regular check-in time of 4 p.m.

I smiled back and said, "Yes, I understand. I was wondering if you could help me. I totally forgot about the 4 p.m. check-in time and I have a business meeting I would love to get freshened up for that starts at 2 p.m. I'm pretty stinky from traveling for 10 hours and it would be a dream if I could somehow find a place to shower before then. Do you have any ideas?" I gave her a big smile, with eyebrows raised and hands clasped in prayer position.

She perked up her chest, began typing away, and said, "Let me see what I can do!" After a minute she said, "I'll tell you what. I have a Royal Oceanfront suite that's empty right now. It's four categories higher in price than the room you have reserved, but since it's not booked, and you need to get into a room, I'll let you stay there for the week at no extra charge."

ALOHA! Royal Oceanfront it was. The view, the huge living room, the kitchenette, and second bathroom! Say things nicely and you might get more than you ask for.

*"The single biggest problem in communication is the illusion that it has taken place."*
- George Bernard Shaw

# 9

# Dating Superpowers

> *"Love is a friendship set to music."*
> -Joseph Campbell

I used to date the wrong way, which led to many broken hearts. But once I started dating the right way, it became way more fun! It was like I had superpowers — I could instantly tell if someone was wrong for me. Even better, I could tell when they were right for me.

Are you ready for the dating superpower? Here it is: *Wait until marriage to go all the way*. I know it sounds lame, but let me tell you why it's awesome. When I dated the wrong way, my body tricked my brain into thinking, "This guy is perfect for me," and "I love him!" But that was just my hormones talking. I made the mistake of thinking I could marry this one guy I dated, but if you took the physical part out, we were not a match at all. I was an adventurer, a mover and a shaker. He was extremely cute but had no motivation. Everyone else could see it but me. We would have driven each other crazy. If we had a baby (which is another reason why you want to wait for marriage), it would not have turned out well!

Now, I'm not perfect. I've made many mistakes in this area. When I was younger, I sought validation through boys, only to feel disappointed when the relationship didn't last. I went from relationship to relationship, each time ending brokenhearted.

One day, while sitting in church, I heard the pastor say, "You need to be in a life group with people your age and in your stage of life." Intrigued, I decided to join a small group of single girls led by a wonderful newly-married woman named Erin. During one of our meetings, Erin introduced the topic for the night: Celibacy.

"Celibacy? What's that?" I asked. Erin then explained the benefits of waiting until marriage to go all the way.

I had faintly heard of this concept before but never had a friend talk about it, nor did I fully understand what the benefits were. She shared that when you wait to have sex until marriage, you can think clearly and recognize whether you really like the person or not. It protects your heart from the ups and downs that come with sexual relationships, especially if one of you is not ready for commitment. You avoid catching sexually transmitted diseases and avoid unplanned pregnancies. You also gain more respect for yourself. She ended by saying, "If a guy leaves because you don't want to go all the way, then he isn't the one for you."

I decided to try it out! I went out on a few dates with some very handsome guys and my new superpowers started to work. As we got to know each other deeper, I realized that our values about family and finances were completely different and I could see problems arising in the future. When we decided to part ways, my emotions were not tangled up because all we did was kiss and it was easy to say goodbye.

Then I met David. We met online and decided to have our first date at Starbucks inside a Barnes and Noble. His big blue eyes, charming smile, and confident swagger swept me away. We talked for hours and over the next few weeks we became inseparable. Then came New Year's Eve. He invited me to go to a party at his best friend's house and since it was New Year's Eve, and there might be drunk drivers on the road, we were invited to spend the night in his friend's guest room together. I was afraid to tell David that I was waiting for marriage because I didn't want to scare him away. But I remembered what Erin said, so I mustered up the courage to tell him that I was being celibate and then there was a long pause. Then he finally replied, "Oh, thank goodness! I honestly would prefer to wait. As a guy, I have always felt social pressure to go faster, but truthfully I would prefer to get to know the real you first." He shared how he had dated girls in the past, only to find out that there was a total personality clash after they went all the way. He wanted to get out, but he felt stuck. We talked all day and all night and got to know each other on a deeper level. Six months later we were married!

**Girls:** There is a famous saying, "Why buy the cow if the milk is free?" If you give up all the goods, it won't last long. I heard this saying many times and thought it was stupid ... until I tried it and it worked! You are truly valuable and a good man will see it.

**Guys:** My comedian husband David likes to say, "Don't buy the cow based on the size of her udder! You need to find out if the cow is healthy on the inside because that determines if the milk is sweet or sour. You don't want to spend a lifetime drinking sour milk, do you?"

## Bring Your Whole Self

Another superpower in dating is to "bring your whole self" into the relationship. This means not expecting your partner to fill any gaps in your life. Instead, focus on being happy and fulfilled on your own. When you're complete by yourself, you're not relying on someone else to make you happy. We're all human and imperfect, so expecting someone to be perfect and make you whole will only lead to disappointment.

By being whole, you'll create a healthier relationship where you support each other without the pressure of being responsible for the other's happiness. Together, you can build a strong, balanced, and fulfilling partnership.

LIZ LEQUEUX

My friend Erica married the man of her dreams. When they had a baby it became very hard for her to be alone all day taking care of the baby while her husband was at work. He didn't like to be away from the family, but they had to pay the bills. She grew lonely and depressed being stuck inside the house all day and began to blame him for her misery.

One day, she was listening to a motivational audiobook by Jim Rohn and heard him say, "I'll take care of me for you, if you'll take care of you for me." What he means is, if you take care of yourself — your health, spirituality, nutrition, and filling your time with fun and friends — you will be a happier person to be around and vice versa. That concept was eye-opening for her!

Erica decided to join Stroller Strides, a moms group where you take your baby to the park and do exercises together pushing your baby around in the stroller. She met a ton of new friends she could relate to and went out to lunch with them every day. By the time her husband got home, Erica was a happy person and was excited to see him.

## Relationship Kryptonite

One element that weakens the bond between couples is something I call "relationship kryptonite." It's different for men and women. When a man's relational needs do not get met, he can become cold, distant, and short with his words. When a woman's relational needs do not get met, she can become critical, controlling, and withhold physical affection.

What are the relational needs of men and women? Dr. Emerson Eggerichs wrote a great book called, *Love and Respect: The Love She Most Desires; The Respect He Desperately Needs.* Dr. Eggerichs writes how women need love to feel happy, and men need respect. The book explains that when these needs aren't met, couples can end up in constant arguments and misunderstandings, called the "Crazy Cycle." By learning to show love and respect to each other, couples can break this cycle and build a happier, healthier relationship.

My husband David has been helping his friend Connor with his marriage. Connor says, "Avery and I were super happy at the beginning of our marriage, but now all we do is fight about the smallest things." The root of the problem was deeper than these surface issues. Connor had landed a new job as an account executive, which demanded a lot of his energy throughout the day. By the time he got home, he was so exhausted that he just wanted to decompress alone before spending time with Avery. She understood how tired he was, so she let him rest while she caught up on her emails. When they did spend time together, he was distant and quiet.

As Connor acquired more accounts, he found himself taking important business calls during dinner many nights, and by the time he finished his calls, Avery was already upstairs getting ready for bed. She was understanding about his work, but her love language was quality time, and she began to grow impatient. When Connor tried to snuggle up to her at night, she found herself turning a cold shoulder, even though she missed him. During dinners with their friends, she'd roll her eyes when he bragged about his latest golf game and became critical about everything he did. She didn't realize that she was being disrespectful, and thus, the "Crazy Cycle" began.

The lack of love and respect is sometimes so subtle that neglect can creep into your relationship. But if you're aware of the principle that women need love and men need respect, it can save your relationship. My husband shared the concept of Love and Respect with Connor, and he decided to implement it. His work schedule remained the same, but this time he made an effort to tell Avery how beautiful she was and how much he loved her every morning at breakfast. He called her on his lunch break just to tell her he was thinking of her. When he got home from work, instead of decompressing alone, he asked Avery to join him on a walk around the neighborhood to get fresh air, hold hands, and spend time together. She felt so loved that she naturally became more affectionate. Instead of criticizing him, she began to compliment and affirm his actions. The love and respect they showed each other revitalized their marriage.

*"Love is not about how many days, months, or years you've been together. Love is about how much you love each other every single day."*
-Unknown

**10**

# Your Superhero Squad

*"Surround yourself with positive people who believe in your dreams, encourage your ideas, support your ambitions, and bring out the best in you."*
-Roy T. Bennett

In the movie *Avengers: Infinity War*, the battle against Thanos demanded the united strength and abilities of all the Avengers, as no single hero could defeat him alone. Much like this iconic team, our own lives are significantly impacted by the support systems we build around us. Our friends, family, mentors, and colleagues form our very own "superhero squad." With their combined strength, wisdom, and encouragement, we are empowered to face challenges and achieve greatness. Life is not meant to go alone. Together, we become unstoppable.

In today's digital age, it's easy to feel connected to so many people through so many channels but so lonely and isolated at the same time. It's important for us to find our "superhero squad" or our "tribe" to maintain good mental health and go on the journey of life together. These are people who share our values, beliefs, and perspectives. They will understand us, support us, and cheer us on. Finding our squad means finding a sense of belonging and connection that enriches our lives and helps us thrive.

I've had a different squad for each chapter of my life. First, I joined a wonderful group of single girls from my church who supported me through my single days. We laughed together, cried together, and went out on the town together. We kept each other company until we all eventually met our match and got married.

When I became a mom, I joined a moms group that helped me through the hardest stage in my life — figuring out how to take care of these precious little lives I was now responsible for! Ashley, Alesia, Robin, Taylor, Jen, Susan, and Paula carried me through and spoke into my life. We got together for playdates, taught each other life hacks for parenting, and brought meals to each other when someone had a baby. Those Wednesday mornings were truly treasured.

At the beginning of my career, I joined an incredible team that mentored, coached, and nurtured my growth in the business. I found like-minded friends — Sean, Loren, Mike, Tracy, Haas, Gerry, Sallie, and Emeline — who all desired a better life and were willing to work hard and make sacrifices to achieve our goals together. We locked arms and have cheered each other on throughout the journey.

On this same team, I found amazing mentors — Brian, Elizabeth, and Fard — who taught me success principles, leadership skills, financial strategies to multiply my money, and how to reach new levels of achievement.

Today, I lead a team of thousands of amazing leaders who are making a positive impact on the world every day.

Joining a group of people with common interests and goals will help you succeed on the journey of life. My mentor and best-selling author, Brian Carruthers, wrote the book *Got GAME?* which stands for:

**G**reat
**A**ssociations
**M**entors and
**E**nvironment

If you are associated with positive people, find great mentors, and you're in a winning environment, you will have the support system you need to thrive.

## Who Will You Put On Your Squad?

Friends are wonderful! They lift us up when we're down, share inside jokes that make us laugh forever, and let us be ourselves because they love us for who we are. Friends also have the power to influence us, both positively and negatively. As the saying goes, "You will become the average of the five people you spend the most time with." The question is: What kind of person do you want to become?

If you hang out with five people who drink energy drinks, you will most likely end up drinking energy drinks. If you hang out with five people who invest their money, you will most likely learn how to invest your money. If you hang out with five people who get in trouble all the time, you will most likely end up in a situation where you get into trouble.

**5 Questions To Ask Yourself About Your Friends:**

*What do they have me doing?*
*What do they have me saying?*
*What do they have me reading?*
*What do they have me seeing?*
*What do they have me listening to?*

## Avoid Toxic People

These are people who have a consistently negative impact on your life and well-being. They might make you feel bad about yourself, constantly criticize you, or create unnecessary drama and stress. Being around toxic people can be emotionally draining and make it hard for you to stay positive or feel confident.

Although we want to love and accept everyone for who they are, it doesn't mean you need to spend a lot of time with them if it drains you.

A lady I used to work with at the pizza shop used to mumble under her breath a lot, "I don't like this guy, look at his hair." When I rang the man up for his pizza, he was a really nice guy! Another time she said, "Stay away from that lady, she is weird." When I served her table, she turned out to be the sweetest lady! This coworker of mine was negative, and mean and criticized everyone she saw.

If Michelle has a problem with Andy ...

and Michelle has a problem with Jayden ...

and Michelle has a problem with Cassie ...

then Michelle might be the problem!

You will meet many friends throughout your life. The beauty is you get to choose who you want to spend more time with and who you recognize you should spend less time with.

## Where to Find Positive People to Surround Yourself With

1. **Life Groups:** Many churches and places of worship have life groups you can join, tailored to your age or stage of life.

2. **Networking Groups:** Search for networking groups in your area by simply Googling "networking groups near me." These can be great groups to find positive, like-minded friends.

3. **Interest-Based Groups:** Look for groups that share your interests, such as hiking, running, tennis, pickleball, basketball, soccer, skiing, dancing, weightlifting, cycling, martial arts, gaming, fishing, traveling, cooking, crafting, volunteering, stocks, real estate, and more.

4. **Home-Based Business Opportunities:** Consider joining a home-based business. These opportunities allow you to earn income while being in a positive, encouraging environment with like-minded friends.

5. **Volunteer Organizations:** Volunteer for local charities, non-profits, or community service projects

to meet others who are passionate about making a difference.

By exploring these options, you can surround yourself with positive and supportive people who will inspire and uplift you.

*"Two are better than one ... If either of them falls down, one can help the other up. But pity anyone who falls and has no one to help them up ... Though one may be overpowered, two can defend themselves. A cord of three strands is not quickly broken."*
(Ecclesiastes 4:9-12)

# 11

# Dreams

> *"Setting goals is the first step in turning the invisible into the visible."*
> –Tony Robbins

A 1953 graduating class of Harvard MBA students were asked if they had goals.

3% said they wrote their goals down.

13% said they had goals, just not written down.

84% said they did not have goals at all.

Ten years later, the 13% who had goals but didn't write them down earned on average twice as much as the

84% who did not have goals at all. The 3% who wrote their goals down outperformed everyone altogether by earning ten times as much as all of the other 97% combined!

So, writing your goals down sounds like a good idea, doesn't it? My coach, David Byrd, the author of *Achievement*, said, "You can have anything you want in life if you're willing to write it down and plan it out!"

My goal was to be financially free, pay off my debt, and meet Mr. Right. So I wrote down "I am a financially free fiance!"

I wrote it down on 10 pieces of paper and taped up copies everywhere in my house. I taped it to my bathroom mirror, my microwave, my desk, and the car dashboard. Everywhere I turned it said, "I am a financially free fiance." Friends would come over and giggle, "What is this all about?"

It was funny but I was reminded every day of where I was going. On days I felt sad or lost, I would see it, regain hope, and keep moving forward. Because I kept seeing it, I eventually became financially free, paid off the debt and, yes, I met Mr. Right!

**What are your goals this year for your:**

Relationships _____
_____

Health _____
_____

Career _____
_____

Finances _____
_____

Fun _____
_____

Faith _____
_____

My Goal for this year: _____
_____
_____
_____

Why is this goal important to you? _____
_____
_____
_____
_____

If you want to have a deeper meaning of purpose in your goal, you need to know why it's important for you to achieve it. What will achieving this do to better your life? Will it also help your family or a loved one? Will it help solve problems in your community or in the world?

Let's re-write your goal and combine it with your "why."

My Goal this year is to _____
so that (insert your why) _____
_____

Everyone has dreams ... it's the ones who take the time to plan them out that make them come to life.

> *"A goal without a plan is just a wish."*
> -Antoine de Saint- Exupery

## Visualize Your Success

My youngest son, Maxwell, is learning about the presidents of the United States in his second-grade class. Recently, he told me that he wants to be the president when he grows up! Every day, when he comes home from school, he takes off his play clothes and puts on his little six-piece suit that was passed down from his cousin — gray pants, a white button-down shirt, a pinstripe vest, a gray jacket, a black tie, and a red handkerchief. He stands behind the desk in my office and practices his presidential speech into my big Yeti microphone, waving his right hand in the air. I have no doubt that he will grow up to be the president (or at least the president of a big company). That or a pastor!

When I decided I was ready to get married, I called my best friend and said, "Judith, I'm getting married!"

In shock, she replied, "To whom? You're not dating anyone right now!" I was single but determined to find Mr. Right. I ran out to Target and bought a big 2' x 3' poster board, two bridal magazines, scissors, and glue. I cut out pictures of the perfect wedding day and pasted them to the board. It had a gorgeous white satin wedding dress, bright fuchsia bridesmaid dresses, a five-tower cake, a hot groom (taller and slimmer than I'm normally attracted to), and a platinum princess-cut engagement ring. I hung it up next to my bedroom closet and saw it every day when I got dressed. It was a fun vision board to fantasize and dream about.

A few months later, I started going on dates, so I hid the board away in my closet in case I ever showed a guy around my condo. I didn't want guys to think I was one of those crazy or obsessed girls planning out their wedding (even though that's exactly what I did! LOL.)

A year later, I was married (you know that story from Chapter 9) and as I was packing to move to David's house, I found the vision board. I was shocked when I looked at it. The engagement ring on my finger (out of hundreds of different shapes, sizes, and colors he could have chosen) was the same exact platinum princess-cut ring! The groom on the poster board looked just like David — taller and slimmer than I was used to dating. We had the wedding with bridesmaids in bright fuschia, my white satin dress, and the five-tower cake.

> "What you vividly imagine, ardently desire, sincerely believe, and enthusiastically act upon must inevitably come to pass."
>
> -Paul J. Meyer
> Founder of Success Motivation Institute

## The Power of Planning

I recommend you get a day planner. I can't live without mine. When I fill out my planner, it's my strong self saying to my weak self, "Just do this and you'll get there!"

When I meet someone who says "I don't know how I'm going to get it all done" or "I'm feeling overwhelmed and anxious about all the things I have to do swirling in my head," as soon as they start using a planner, all those fears and worries go away. Using a planner helps you make a space and time for each item to get done.

**How To Use Your Day Planner:**

**1. Take your goal for the year and break it down into monthly plans.**

For example: You wish to run a 26.2 mile marathon one year from now. Your first month's plan is to run up to three miles. Your second month's plan is to run up to five miles. Your third month's plan is to run up to seven miles and so on until your last month you're ready to run a marathon of 26.2 miles.

What are monthly plans to get you to your goal: _____
_____
_____
_____
_____

**2. Determine your daily action steps that will get you to your goal.**

For example: To train properly for your marathon you'll need to hydrate and drink 10 glasses of water a day, run every other day, and meal prep the night before so you can eat properly when you're on the go.

What are daily action steps that will get you to your goal: _____
_____
_____
_____
_____

**3. Schedule a time in your planner to get these daily action steps done.**

For example: Run from 7 a.m.-8 a.m. Set my alarm to go off every hour to drink a glass of water, and meal prep every day at 6 p.m.

What time will you get these action steps done? _____
_____
(Now transfer these to your planner.)

**4. Before you end each day, plan out your next one.**

Coach David Byrd said, "Plan for the day before the next day begins." He was right! When I planned for the next day before I went to bed, I'd wake up, follow the plan, and crush the day! When I forgot to plan for the next day, I'd wake up and wander through it, slightly lost. Before you close up shop for the day, write down your action plan for tomorrow.

## How Can You Tell If Your Dream Is From God?

Because I am involved in ministry, people often ask me, "I have my own goals, but how can I tell if this dream was given to me by God?"

Pastor Rick Warren, who wrote *The Purpose Driven Life*, says, "You'll know your dream is from God if it involves helping people." Most of Jesus's miracles and teachings were about helping people.

My daughter Lilly has the dream of becoming a professional singer. She has the most beautiful voice. She sings in the junior high church band and uses her music to comfort teens going through hard times and inspiring them to do good. In a world where many artists glorify negative behavior, Lilly's dream is to be a beacon of positivity. She's becoming the change the world needs to see.

So if your goal involves helping people, you're on the right track. If it isn't yet, ask yourself how you can use your dream to help people.

*"Don't conform to the patterns of this world, but be transformed by the renewing of your mind."*
(Romans 12:2)

# 12

# Your Unique Superpower

*"To laugh often and much; to win the respect of intelligent people and the affection of children; to earn the appreciation of honest critics and endure the betrayal of false friends; to appreciate beauty; to find the best in others; to leave the world a bit better, whether by a healthy child, a garden patch, or a redeemed social condition; to know even one life has breathed easier because you have lived. This is to have succeeded."*
                                                              -Ralph Waldo Emerson

Each superhero has his or her own unique power. Thor has the power of thunder. Hulk has the power of SMASH! Wonder Woman holds the lasso of truth, and YOU have a superpower, too.

My business partner Dawn Brinkley loves telling people what their superpower is … and that's her superpower! She says:

"Melody, your superpower is drawing people to you. You are magnetic!"

"Sylvia, your superpower is that you can always find someone to help you no matter where you are. You are sweet and lovable!"

"Patrick, your superpower is you give off an aura of trust. You are trustworthy!"

"Betty, random people just talk to you at length and you listen and give great advice. You are endearing!"

My superpower is encouraging people and making them feel loved. I gave myself a superhero name "Chief Encouragement Officer."

REAL WORLD SUPERPOWERS

## What's your superpower?

My Superpowers: _____

_____

_____

What do you enjoy doing or are good at? (Circle)

- Acting
- Advocating
- Analytical Thinking
- Artistic Ability
- Athleticism
- Baking
- Budgeting
- Carpentry
- Coaching
- Coding
- Communication Skills
- Cooking
- Creativity
- Critical Thinking
- Dancing
- Drawing
- Emotional Intelligence
- Entrepreneurial
- Event Planning
- Gardening
- Graphic Design
- Innovative
- Investigating
- Leadership
- Listening Skills
- Loyal
- Mathematical Ability
- Mentoring
- Musical Talent
- Negotiation Skills
- Organizational Skills
- Painting
- Persuading
- Photography

- Problem-Solving
- Protecting
- Public Speaking
- Researching
- Representing
- Selling
- Sewing
- Social Media
- Social Skills
- Storytelling

- Teaching
- Tech Savvy
- Time Management
- Trustworthy
- Writing
- _____
- _____
- _____

You fill in the blanks!

You are a unique gift to this world with a special dream placed inside of you by God. He planned your life long before you were born. Your parents may not have planned you, but He did. He created you to do good on this Earth and gave you the gifts to succeed in your dream. Even if you're unsure of your dream, that stirring inside you is Him calling you to step into your greatness!

The Bible says, "I know the plans I have for you, declares the Lord, plans to prosper you and not to harm you, plans to give you hope and a future." — Jeremiah 29:11

No matter where you come from, what you're going through, or the mistakes you've made, when you accept the love that God brought to this Earth by sending His son, Jesus, for you to receive, you will live an empowered life of fulfillment and joy. You may have felt mistreated or misunderstood growing up. There were times when I did not feel loved for who I was. What gave me the courage to believe in myself was knowing that we are all unconditionally loved by God (Jeremiah 31:3). In today's social media age, it's easy to forget this and feel inadequate, constantly comparing yourself to others. But remember, Jesus' love for you is not based on your followers, likes, or accomplishments. It's based on who you are and you don't need to prove anything to earn His love — it's already yours.

> **If you're relying on people to tell you your worth, you'll always be disappointed. If you look to God, you will be reminded daily how incredibly worthy you are!**

## So what will YOU be about?

You will influence many people in your lifetime. No matter how big or small your role, everyone influences someone — even if it's just your little brother. So, what will you be about?

Choosing what you're going to be about in life is a big deal. Think about the kind of influence you want to have on the world. Do you want to be known for abusive behavior like the infamous singer P. Diddy, or would you prefer to be like Chris Pratt from "Guardians of the Galaxy," who uses his platform to support various charitable causes, including children's hospitals and providing clean water to communities in need? Both stars influence people, but it's important to consider what kind of impact you'll have on others. Strive to be someone who lifts people up, inspires positive change, and leaves a lasting legacy of goodness. Your choices today will shape the person you become and the mark you leave on the world. So, choose wisely and aim to be the best version of yourself.

## Be The Change You Want To See

Don't wait for others to fix things. The next time you see something at work, school, or your club that bugs you, don't wait for leadership to fix it. They have enough on their plate. Be the change you want to see. Create the solution and implement it. If God gave you the vision that things could be better, that means He gave you the ability to make them better.

My mentor Brian Carruthers always taught me, "If you have a problem, don't just call your leader and say, 'Here's my problem.' Instead, call and say, 'Here's my problem and here is a possible solution. What do you think?'" Eventually, you won't call with problems because you've already solved them!

*"We are not on earth to see how important we can become, but to see how much difference we can make in the lives of others."*
-Gordon Hinckley, Author of *Stand for Something*

## Your Ripple Effect

What you choose to do can have a ripple effect. Robert and Susan Joseph, entrepreneurs from Orlando, FL, ignited a positive movement by deciding to grow and develop leaders. They developed a great leader, Elsie Mendez, inspiring her to dedicate herself to mentoring others and transforming their lives. One of the individuals Elsie mentored was Glenda Orellana, who extended her teachings to the Spanish community. Glenda's efforts are now providing hope and opportunities to hundreds of people! The ripple effect initiated by Robert and Susan continues to impact countless lives, many of whom they may never know.

At the end of our lives, what we most regret are the things we didn't do. My first realtor, Bob Smith, once told me, "Liz, it's easy to be successful because most people aren't trying." I hold onto this advice every time I'm about to create something new or put myself out there. His words encourage me to go for it when I'm about to second-guess myself or worry about what others might think.

Bob passed away shortly after sharing this wisdom, and while I miss him, thinking about his life brings a smile to my face. He lived a full and happy life, always chasing his dreams. He didn't sit around letting life pass him by; he lived with purpose.

> **It's easy to be successful because most people aren't trying!**
> - Bob Smith

*THIS!*

Have the courage to embrace God's calling for your life! Even if you don't see the entire picture right now, that's perfectly OK. Writing this book was never something I planned when I first ventured out into the world. Yet, everything I've done in my life has prepared me to write it for you today. You might only be aware of what you're being called to do right now, but I'm thrilled for you to take that step and put it into action. Your life is destined to make a significant difference in this world.

Embrace your uniqueness and let your light shine. Just like superheroes, you have the power to make a difference. Believe in yourself and never let anyone tell you that you can't achieve greatness. Your journey is special, and your potential is limitless. Remember, the world needs your superpower.

> *"Anything is possible if a person believes."*
> (Mark 9:23)

# Commencement Speech

Dear Superhero,

Now that you have unlocked these superpowers, you are ready and equipped to navigate challenges and seize big opportunities!

**Believe in yourself.** Don't wait for others to believe in you. You must be the first one. Believe in your mission if you don't know how to believe in yourself. *Remember, you were created for a great purpose that only you can fulfill.*

**Don't take things personally.** As leaders, you will face criticism, setbacks, and obstacles. Understand that the negative comment is more about the person who is dishing it than the person receiving it. Maintain your focus, and stay resilient! *You are stronger than the obstacles that come your way.*

**Take initiative and action.** The world is full of opportunities waiting for those who are willing to seize them. Be proactive, take risks, show up early and stay late. Great leaders do not wait for things to happen; they make things happen. Be bold and take charge of your destiny. *You have the power to create a positive impact on the world.*

**Take responsibility for your life and your choices.** By taking responsibility, you empower yourself to make positive changes. Remember, you are the author of your own story, and it is up to you to write the chapters. *You hold the pen to your life's narrative.*

**Choose the glass half full.** Your perspective on life can significantly impact your happiness and success. Embrace optimism and look for the silver lining in everything you do and the goodness in everyone you meet. Your positive outlook can light the way for others.

**Use your Rizz!** Relationships are the key to a fulfilling life. Use your charisma to listen, understand, and genuinely care for others. *You can make a difference in someone's life.*

**Choose your right mate wisely.** The people you surround yourself with, especially your life partner, play a crucial role in your journey. Seek a partner who supports your dreams, encourages your growth, and shares your values. Together, you can build a life filled with love, joy, and purpose. *Together, you can conquer any challenge!*

**Go for your dreams.** Do what sets your soul on fire. Your unique superpower was given to you to make a difference in the world. *God will only give you dreams that you can handle!*

In closing, remember that *leadership is not about power, but about how many lives you can empower.* I love you and I believe in you. You are now equipped with everything you need to succeed.

THE WORLD NEEDS YOUR LEADERSHIP.
**Now go save the world!**

If you enjoyed reading this, please leave a review on Amazon. I read every review and they help new readers discover my books.

For more motivation and daily encouragement from Liz visit www.LizLeq.com or subscribe to her YouTube ministry
www.YouTube.com/@CEOLizLeq